SUPERBASE 19
DIJON

SUPERBASE 19

DIJON

The Mirage Masters

John Blackman

Acknowledgements

Whilst only one name appears on the cover it is a fact that a book like this could never appear without the help and co-operation of a great number of people. I am indebted to the *Chef d'Etat-Major de l'Armée de l'Air* for granting their permission and to Colonel J Rolland and Lt Col S Lenne of SIRPA-AIR for arranging facilities.

The personnel of BA 102 went out of their way to be both hospitable and helpful and sincere thanks are due to all those who found themselves in front of my lens. But of those that avoided that dubious pleasure there are several who deserve individual mention; Colonel Brugnon – Base Commander, Lt Col Imberti – 2nd *Escadre* Commander, Commandant Garrot – Commander GERMAS 15.002 and Lieutenant Debèvre – BA 102 Public Relations.

I am particularly grateful to Lt Col Labaye, Captain Murray Carlsson and Lieutenant Nicolas Romanoff, all of whom gave me the benefit of their time and experience, as did Lt Col Boissonnet and Commandant Lardet of ERV 1/93 at Istres.

Finally, I thank my lucky stars to have had as guide, translator and downright good company, Aspirant Damian Motte. All photographs were taken with Olympus cameras and my thanks go to Ian Dickens and Olympus Optical UK Ltd for the loan of equipment used.

Published in 1991 by Osprey Publishing Limited
59 Grosvenor Street, London W1X 9DA

© John Blackman 1991

British Library Cataloguing in Publication Data

Blackman, John, *1948* —
    Superbase 19 Dijon.
    1. France, Armée de l'Air aerodromes
    I. Title
    358.417094442

ISBN 1855 321130

Editor Tony Holmes
Page design Paul Kime
Printed in Hong Kong

For a catalogue of all books published by Osprey Aerospace please write to:

The Marketing Manager, Consumer Catalogue Department Osprey Publishing Ltd, 59 Grosvenor Street, London, W1X 9DA

Above Caught in the evocative light of an autumn afternoon, a Mirage 2000C of EC 3/2 'Alsace' taxies past an ATC radar installation. Operational control of the 2nd *Escadre de Chasse*, consisting of three squadrons and a second line maintenance unit, is the responsibility of *Commandment Air des Forces de Défence Aérienne* (CAFDA). The base, however, falls under the jurisdiction of *Force Aérienne Tactique* (FATac). It is their responsibility to provide the 2nd *Escadre* with the means necessary to fulfil their mission as the cutting edge of France's air defence network; air traffic control, building works and ground-to-air defence are just some of the jobs performed by FATac

Title page The Dassault-Breguet Mirage 2000, a totally French designed and built thoroughbred. Fly-by-wire controls, a variable camber wing and integrated radar, weapons and navigation systems help to ensure that this chic delta can mix it with the best. First recipients of the aircraft were the 2nd *Escadre de Chasse* (EC 2) based at BA 102 '*Guynemer*' at Dijon-Longvic. EC 2 arrived at Dijon from Germany in 1949 to fly their first jet aircraft, the Vampire. Since then they have converted successively to the Ouragan in 1953, Mystere IV in 1956, Mirage III in 1961 and since 1984, the Mirage 2000

Front cover Positioning himself for a run in at the boom, a Mirage 2000 trainee pilot looks to be in the right position to commence the manoeuvre. Attached to *Escadrille SPA 94*, this Mirage 2000B is in typical Dijon 'OCU' configuration

Back cover Crewed by Commandant Switzer, an EC 1/2 Mirage 2000C is enveloped in sunshine as it taxies out of its protective shelter

Introduction

France occupies the largest landmass of any European country, but although an economic and military world power, it no longer boasts the largest air force in the world as it arguably could at the end of World War 1. But make no mistake, today's *Armée de l'Air* packs a mighty punch.

Lying south-east of Paris is the *Bourgogne* or Burgundy region. Steeped in a tradition of gastronomic excellence, a gazetteer of the area reads like a cross between a fine wines list and good food guide. But Dijon, capital of the area, is more than a stopping off point for lovers of a well stocked table; it is a natural crossroads. To the west, the heartland of France, to the east, a short hop to the borders of Switzerland, Italy and Germany. Dijon was an obvious location for the fledgling *Aviation Militaire*, as it was then known, to base one of their first aerial observation units in 1912. Two years later an airbase was officially inaugurated in the suburb of Longvic, a couple of miles south of the historic centre of Dijon.

It was there on 13 May 1916 that the famous ace Guynemer was presented with the first flag of the *Armée de l'Air*. A year later Capitaine Guynemer disappeared whilst on a mission over Belgium, having attained 53 confirmed kills and legendary status. Such was his fame that news of his death was delayed for fear of the effect on national morale.

Today both the flag and the Guynemer legend live on at the renamed BA 102 *Base Aérienne 'Guynemer'*, home of the 2nd *Escadre de Chasse* and linchpin of France's air defence network. Whilst the *Armée de l'Air*, and the personnel of BA 102 in particular, look back with justifiable pride at the example set by Guynemer and his contemporaries, there is no question that they look to the future as far as current operations are concerned.

From the very start the *Armée de l'Air* has made a concerted effort to equip with indigenous aircraft, and to ensure those aircraft are a match for anything available elsewhere. Guynemer's Spad was very much state-of-the-art, 1916 style, as unwary German Albatros pilots patrolling the Western Front soon found out. Likewise, the sleek Mirage 2000 is state-of-the-art 1990's style, this beauty being able to turn and burn and slip and slide with the best.

So let's take a walk down the Dijon flightline for a closer look at the men and machines, the *créme de la créme*, of the *Armée de l'Air*.

Below The author finds an excuse to get himself in on the act!

Contents

Below The Guynemer monument. In 1916 the names of Georges Guynemer, *Escadron 'Cigognes'* (Storks) and Dijon-Longvic became inextricably linked. Guynemer was a pale young man battling with the debilitating effects of tuberculosis who had joined the *Aviation Militaire* after being declared unfit to serve his country in the trenches. Flying with *Escadrille* (flight) 3 of the *'Cigognes'* squadron, he proved to be a brilliant fighter pilot, driving himself to the edge of exhaustion whilst fast building a reputation as one of France's leading aces

Combatant Converter

One by one the needle-nosed Mirage 2000Bs of *Escadron de chasse et de Transformation* (ECT) 2/2 *'Côte d'Or'* are towed out onto the BA 102 *'Guynemer'* flightline at the start of another day's flying. A groundcrewman vacates the hot seat and gives the screen one last polish before climbing down and disconnecting the towbar. ECT 2/2 *'Côte d'Or'* is unusual in that it consists of three flights rather than the *Armée de l'Air's* routine pair. The trio consists of SPA 57 *'Mouette'* (Seagull), SPA 65 *'Chimére'* (Dragon) and SPA 94 *'La mort qui fauche'* (Grim Reaper)

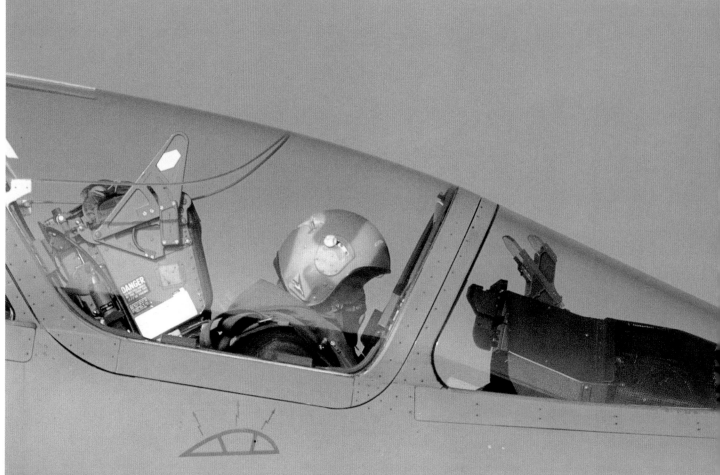

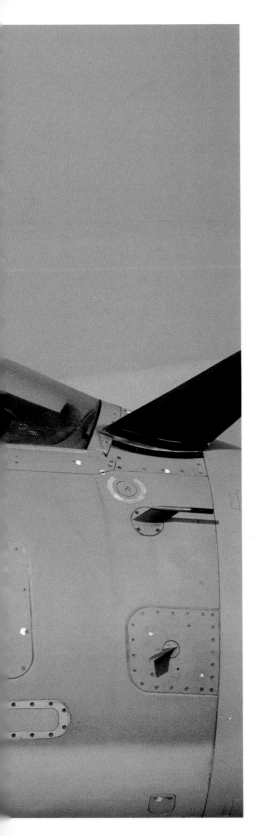

Below A thumbs up from the groundcrew completes the external pre-flight checks. *'Côte d'Or'* was originally formed in October 1949 as EC 3/2 but became EC 2/2 when the 2nd *Escadre de Chasse* reorganized in May 1951. It disbanded on 1 November 1957 but reformed as the Mirage III operational conversion unit in April 1965, and has remained in an OCU role ever since. ECT 2/2 received their first Mirage 2000B on 27 June 1986, becoming the last of the three Dijon squadrons to convert to the new Dassault delta in the process

Left Head down intently scanning his instruments, this pilot probably isn't aware that '2-FA', Dassault-Breguet serial number 502, was the second production Mirage 2000B, and the first delivered to the *Armée de l'Air* when it was sent to the *Centre d'Expérimentation Aériennes Militaire* shortly after its maiden flight on 11 January 1984

Left An impressive and noisy departure by a pair of *'Côte d'Or'* Mirages both bearing the badge of SPA 94 *'La mort qui fauche'*. In the foreground is '2-FL', one of only two single-seat 2000Cs on the ECT 2/2 books. To make room for the additional Martin Baker F10Q zero/zero ejection seat, the Mirage 2000B is eight inches longer than the 47 feet, one and one quarter inch 2000C, carries marginally less internal fuel and lacks the pair of 30 mm DEFA 554 cannon. In all other respects it is fully combat capable

Above With afterburner blazing, this Mirage 2000B's SNECMA M53-5 turbofan is generating almost 20,000 lbs of thrust to blast it into the inviting blue sky at the start of a routine training flight. The 2nd *Escadre de Chasse's* primary mission is air defence, with secondary missions of ground attack and conversion. ECT 2/2 *'Côte d'Or'* fulfil the latter converting pilots, both French and foreign, to the complexities of the Mirage 2000

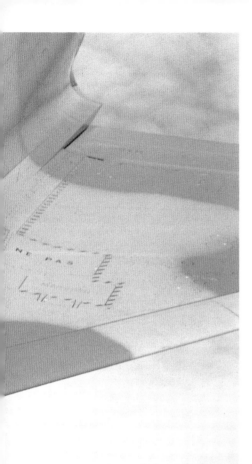

Above Sleek and chic, Dassault-Breguet's finest captured in its element. Mirage 2000B of *Escadrille* SPA 94 *'La mort qui fauche'* gracefully manoeuvres high above patchy cloud over central France. The standard blue/grey air defence camouflage may be the most colourful applied to any European Theatre combat aircraft but it's certainly effective at altitude

Left The pale grey glassfibre radome shrouds a Thomson-CSF RDM multi-mode radar. The same manufacturer also supplied the TMV 980 data display system comprising a VMC 180 head-down display and, visible in this impressive in-flight close-up, a VE 130 head-up display. The fixed strakes near the leading edge of the air intakes stabilize airflow at high angles of attack to improve longitudinal control

Head on and the menacing aspect of the Mirage emerges. This is the last thing an unwelcome intruder in French air space wants to see coming up in his six o'clock. However, no cause for alarm as we're travelling in the belly of a Boeing C-135FR whilst the Mirage 2000B strikes a macho pose in our wake. The wing leading edge slats are partially deployed at this relatively slow speed, far below the Mach 2.2+ that the aircraft is capable of

Above Teaching the art of air refuelling is one of ECT 2/2's major priorities. A fleet of eleven Boeing C-135FR tankers (originally twelve but one was lost over the Pacific in 1972) are operated by *Escadre de Ravitailment en Vol* (ERV) 93, headquartered at Istres, near Marseilles, in southern France. As the heavily laden tanker cruises through air refuelling zone three (26,000 feet above Chateauroux, in central France), a thirsty Mirage 2000B carefully closes in on the drogue. In his headset the Mirage pilot can hear the C-135FR's 'boomer' counting down the distance between probe and drogue; 'Three metres, two metres, one metre . . .'

Right 'Connect!' Valves open and the Mirage 2000B starts to take on fuel at a rate of 1000 lbs a minute. But '2-FI' doesn't swallow the entire 3000 lb allotment in one go. This is a training mission and to extract maximum value the student pilot, under the watchful eye of his instructor, disconnects and reconnects several times whilst maintaining a steady 300 knots

Opposite above Although the *Armée de l'Air* C-135FR tankers retain the USAF style flying boom, the French favour the probe and drogue style of refuelling. The flying boom trails a drogue and the 'boomer' simply lowers it into position, leaving the pilot to drive his aircraft's probe into contact. Whilst one Mirage refuels, another approaches from the tanker's five o'clock low and holds station. He will move across to take a turn once his colleague has topped his tanks and dived away

Opposite below A pair of ECT 2/2 Mirage 2000Bs fly close formation on a C-135FR tanker. ECT 2/2 Mirages are frequently deployed overseas to show the flag, or to take part in Dassault-Breguet's aggressive marketing campaigns. For instance, in February 1990 a pair of '*Côte d'Or*' Mirages flew out to appear at the Singapore International Airshow. They clocked a trouble free 28 hours flight time and 15 in-flight refuellings. The Mirage 2000 has sold to India, Peru, Egypt, Abu-Dhabi, Greece and Jordan, a fitting testament to the aircraft and the service pilots that demonstrate it

Above Even the bolt-on refuelling probe barely mars what is arguably the most aesthetic fighter in service, a 'haute couture' blend of elegance and machismo. The Mirage 2000's fuselage is of conventional metal semi-monocoque construction, with a glass fibre radome. However, much use has been made of carbon fibre material throughout the aircraft, the large avionics bay cover behind the cockpit and the two-section elevons which form the entire trailing edge of each wing being made of light alloy honeycomb, with carbon fibre skinning. Likewise, the tail fin and rudder are largely of composite construction

Below Touch and goes, circuits and bumps, the staple diet of the student pilot. He's concentrating hard, but the instructor allows himself a glance down at the camera. The standard dummy Matra Magic AAM hangs below the starboard outer pylon, this particular round being equipped with a fully operational seeker head to allow the pilot to realistically practice ACM

Opposite above As rear element of the flight, Mirage 2000B '2-FI' pops his chute to avoid the slightest chance of overrunning his leader during a formation landing. With 8000 feet of runway to play with parachutes are not generally used. The aircraft is also capable of carrying an arrestor hook, although the Dijon Mirages don't carry them because the runway has a raisable barrier for emergencies rather than arrestor cables

Opposite below ECT 2/2 '*Côte d'Or*' is unusual in two respects; firstly because it consists of three flights rather than the usual two, and secondly because it applies the same flight badge to both sides of the fin on unit Mirage 2000s. Here we see the grim reaper badge of SPA 94 '*La mort qui fauch*', the flight nickname literally translating to 'the dead with a scythe'

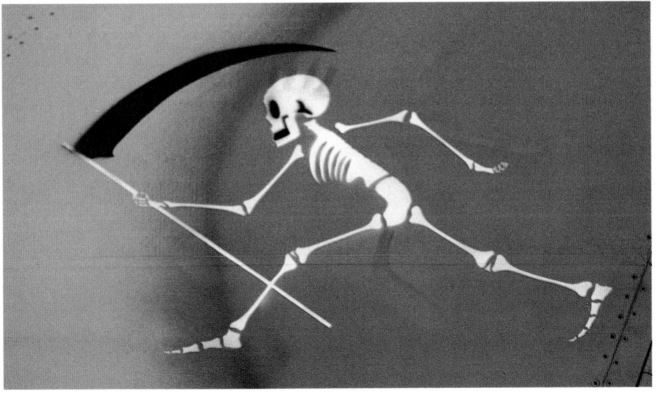

The Indian Air Force call the Mirage 2000 'Vajra' – Divine Thunder, a fitting title for this moody study of heavy metal form and texture taken as storm clouds gathered over RAF Mildenhall, where this ECT 2/2 Mirage 2000B put on a stunning display in May 1989

Above From the rear the Mirage 2000B's distinctive dorsal spine is particularly apparent. The opening half way down the spine is an engine intake by-pass air spill duct, whilst at the very end is the rear high band ECM transmitting aerial. The horizontal mouldings two-thirds of the way up the tailfin contain radar warning and ECM-jamming antennae

Right The Mirage's massive delta wings are swept at an angle of 58 degrees and have two-segment, full span leading edge slats which are deployed automatically to vary camber. In this fashion wing efficiency is optimized throughout the flight envelope. The yellow tipped protrusion visible just inboard of the navigation light is a radar warning antenna

Overleaf Prior to receiving the Mirage 2000 the 2nd *Escadre de Chasse* flew Mirage IIIE and B variants, and were tasked with battlefield air superiority under FATac command. With the arrival of the ultimate Mirage they changed to the air defence role and became subservient to CAFDA. ECT 2/2 *'Côte d'Or'* were the last of the three 2nd *Escadre* squadrons to upgrade to the Mirage 2000, and therefore became the last to change masters, doing so on 1 July 1986

Supersonic Storks

Right Mirage in the mist! Plugged into an auxiliary power supply and temporarily brought to life, a Mirage 2000C of EC 1/2 *'Cigognes'* (Storks) sits becalmed on the fog bound BA 102 *'Guynemer'* flightline. When fog rolls in across the base and scrubs flying for the day an almost palpable depression radiates from the pilot's mess. Revising systems manuals and recognition charts might all be part of the job but sidelong glances out the window tell you where they'd rather be

Below A groundcrewman ensures his pilot straps in tightly. Just visible propped on top of the access ladder is the pilots fancy Mirage decorated bonedome, fashionable wear for the discerning French fighter jock

Left With clear skies and the promise of a good day's flying, groundcrew prepare their squadron's Mirage 2000Cs. Although the Mirage is blessed with a proliferation of electronic aids, there is no substitute for the 'Mk1 eyeball', hence the special attention placed upon cleaning the canopy

Below Following usual *Armée de l'Air* practice, EC 1/2 *'Cigognes'* consists of two flights; SPA 3, whose badge, a stork, wing low, is worn on the left tailfin side; and SPA 103 whose badge, a stork, wing high, we see here. The SPA prefix dates back to World War 1 when the *'Cigognes'* flew the legendary SPAD fighter on the Western Front, the unit attaining a fearsome reputation through the fighting skills of pilots like Georges Guynemer and René Fonck

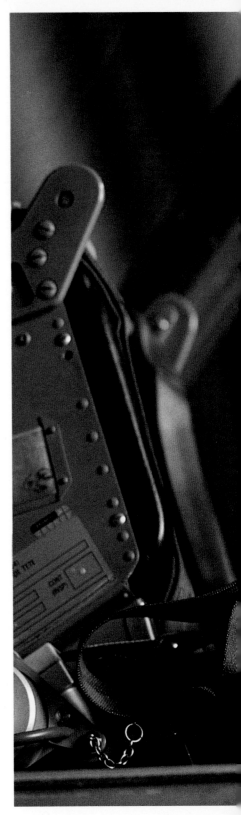

Above left Fully kitted out and with flightsuit pockets bulging, an EC 1/2 pilot conducts a careful walkaround check to satisfy himself that there are no unsecured panels or signs of anything untoward. The webbing straps attached to his leggings clip to the ejector seat and will restrain his legs in the event of an emergency punch out

Above right Today's missions are briefed to the second and run by the clock. *'Cigognes'* pilot, Capitaine Bissiere, takes a glance at his watch before climbing into the cockpit and strapping in. EC 1/2 *'Cigognes'* are arguably the jewel in the *Armée de l'Air* fighter squadron crown. First to receive the Mirage III in 1961, the unit was also the first to come to grips with the Mirage 2000 when they became operational on type on 2 July 1984

Right Capitaine Bissiere proudly wears the *'Cigognes'* squadron insignia velcroed to his flightsuit, and rightly so as EC 1/2 have a pedigree second to none. They bear two of the most famous flight badges in the *Armée de l'Air*, both with origins in World War 1. SPA 3 was the flight with which Capitaine Georges Guynemer scored 54 victories, whilst the highest scoring allied pilot of the war, Capitaine René Fonck, accrued the majority of his 75 confirmed kills with SPA 103. However, it was on 5 January 1944 that the squadron's current term of existence began when Free French pilots were formed into No 329 Squadron of the Royal Air Force, flying Spitfires

Overleaf The universal thumbs up tells us all is well. No sign of leaking fluids, and the control surfaces are moving freely and correctly. The Mirage 2000 is capable of carrying a wide range of external stores under nine hardpoints, but whilst operating on routine missions EC 2 aircraft are likely to carry only a 1300 litre jettisonable fuel tank under the fuselage centre, and a dummy Matra 550 Magic AAM on an outer wing pylon

Left The fighter pilot stare! Strapped into a supersonic dart and ready for action, Capitaine Bissiere fires up his Mirage 2000C in the confines of the hardened aircraft shelter

Below Walking the line, a groundcrewman carefully guides his large charge into the open to perform a series of last minute pre-flight checks. Dassault-Breguet's sleek delta design was selected in December 1975 as the *Armée de l'Air's* future primary combat aircraft. The single-seat prototype's maiden flight took place at Istres on March 10 1978, and the two-seat variant first flew on 11 October 1980

Above Piloted by '*Cigognes*' second-in-command, Commandant Switzer, Mirage 2000C glides out of its shelter prior to flying a two against one air combat mission. Just to even the odds a little the pair will be simulating radio communication problems. His highly stylized helmet, custom painted with storks on a sky blue background, is clearly visible. Though initially developed as an all weather interceptor and air superiority aircraft, the two-seater 2000B has been successfully developed into the 2000N, optimized for the low-level nuclear penetration role

Right '2-EM' heads for Dijon's main runway leaving a wake of hot exhaust gas. As all EC 2 Mirage 2000s are early production aircraft, they are fitted with the SNECMA M53-5 engine rated at 12,230 lbs thrust dry and 19,830 lbs with afterburner. Later deliveries were fitted with the M53-P2, a powerplant with the much improved rating of 14,462 lbs dry and 21,385 lbs wet

Overleaf The Storks fly south. One by one, Mirage 2000Cs of EC 1/2 taxi out to the main runway for take-off, destination Istres. Supersonic flight over mainland France is forbidden under 40,000 ft, but during their two-week long exercise in the south '*Cigognes*' will be able to unleash the Mirage's power over the Mediterranean. 'There is valuable training to be had by being able to go supersonic', explained one pilot, 'particularly in the case of separation from a fight. For example, if you and your partner take out an enemy aircraft in actual combat the explosion in the combat arena attracts everyone within range. So you want to get away from that position as soon as possible, and the Mirage 2000 can move out pretty fast! Over land you can't go supersonic and you lose that training aspect'

Above The badge of Evreux-based *Escadre de Transport* (ET) 64 containing the individual flight badges of ET 1/64 *'Bearn'* and ET 2/64 *'Anjou'*

EC 3/2 *'Alsace'* groundcrew break from their duties to watch one of their squadron aircraft taxi past. Historically speaking EC 3/2 are 'new boys on the block' in that they have no adopted World War 1 *escadrilles*, as have the other two 2nd *Escadre* squadrons. For that reason it is the squadron badge of the Alsace coat of arms that is carried on their aircraft. They formed on 1 January 1943 as No 341 Squadron of the RAF, then returned to the post-war *Armée de l'Air* in November 1945 to form the *Group de Chasse 2* with *'Cigognes'*

Each of the 2nd *Escadre* pilots gets to fly 190 hours a year on average, which might appear to give them plenty of free time. However each mission is preceded by comprehensive briefings. 'We have about three hours from initial briefing to take-off', explained Lieutenant Nicolas Romanoff of EC 3/2 '*Alsace*'. 'We are assigned a target, work out and plot navigation co-ordinates, discuss the mission with our flight leader and at about an hour before take-off we start suiting up'

Below Squadrons are equipped to handle their own first line maintenance. Here, in the EC 3/2 *'Alsace'* hangar, one technician checks out the Martin Baker F10Q zero/zero ejection seat, whilst his colleague lifts the lightweight composite avionics bay cover prior to delving into its complexities

Right 'Flying the Mirage 2000 is the most exhilarating thing I have ever done', said Lieutenant Nicolas Romanoff with conviction. Tragically it was also the last thing he ever did. On January 8 1990, he was killed when his Mirage 2000C crashed into woods near Dijon, a sober reminder of the risks fighter pilots run operating at the leading edge of aviation technology in defence of their country

Above Back from a quick reaction alert scramble, with his Mirage 2000C returned to the safety of it's HAS, you just know from Lt Col Labaye's steely-eyed expression that if they had been playing for keeps there would be one less 'hostile' to worry about. Second-in-command of the 2nd *Escadre*, Lt Col Labaye has been operational since 1976. He has previously flown the Jaguar and Mirage F.1, but is now an unequivocal fan of Dassault-Breguet's latest and greatest. 'Why? Simple, technological improvements. For instance, compared with the Jaguar, which can be a little difficult to fly when fully loaded, the Mirage 2000, with it's fly-by-wire system, gives you good smooth control throughout it's flight envelope. Also, the integrated computerized navigation and weapons systems are a big step forward'

Right Only after signing out his allocated Mirage 2000C in the '*Alsace*' ops room does the pilot get to take the short walk to the HAS and breathe life into the silent machine. After the mandatory walkaround, he will climb the access ladder and, with his crewman's help, strap in

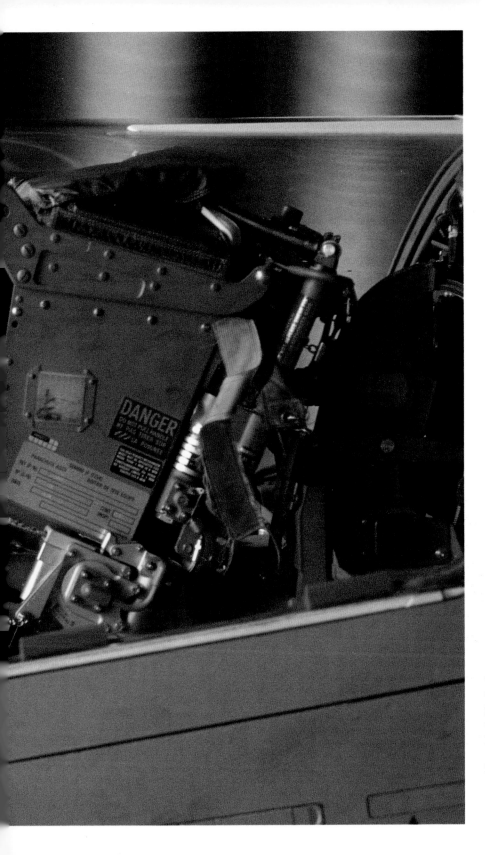

We who are about to fly salute you! The definitive pre-flight portrait. EC 2 battle honours are as impressive as you can get; World War 1 1914–18, France 1940, Libya 1941, Dieppe 1942, Normandy 1944, Germany 1945, Far East 1947, and Suez 1956

Below The pilot of EC 3/2 '*Alsace*' Mirage 2000C '2-LA' gets the thumbs up from his groundcrewman as he prepares to depart on a simulated quick reaction alert (QRA) mission. There's a high-level bogey incoming at Mach 1.7 and he will climb to 42,000 ft to simulate a missile shot. As well as missing out on the uprated SNECMA M53-P2 engine, the 2nd *Escadre's* early production Mirages were also delivered with the Thompson-CSF RDM multi-mode radar rather than the RDI pulse-doppler set. However, there are plans for a retro-fit which will significantly improve the aircraft's all-aspect acquisition capability

Right Accompanied by the distinctive turbofan whine, an '*Alsace*' Mirage 2000C taxies out in the late afternoon light on an unseasonably warm November day. Even from a distance the Mirage III/5 family ancestry is obvious, but beneath the Mirage 2000's alloy and composite skin beats the computerized heart of a completely different aircraft, incorporating a quantum leap in avionics technology

Left Winter sun glinting on metal skins, a pair of '*Alsace*' Mirage 2000Cs roll down less than half of Dijon's 8000 ft main runway before rotating at 140 knots. Typically they will lift at an angle of 15 degrees, cut the afterburner at 250 knots, then lower the nose to five degrees for a smooth climb away

Above In deadly earnest the Mirage 2000 can climb at a maximum rate of 56,000 feet a minute, twice the Mirage III's rate of climb, and is quoted as being able to intercept a hostile target flying at Mach three at 80,000 ft in less than four minutes after a scramble take-off. These two Mirage 2000Cs are carrying the usual training mission external load of 1300 litre fuel tank and dummy Matra Magic, way short of their 13,890 lb maximum external stores weight capability. The most likely configuration for air defence combat would be either four Matra 550 Magics, or a mixture of two Magics and two of the long range Matra 530D AAMs

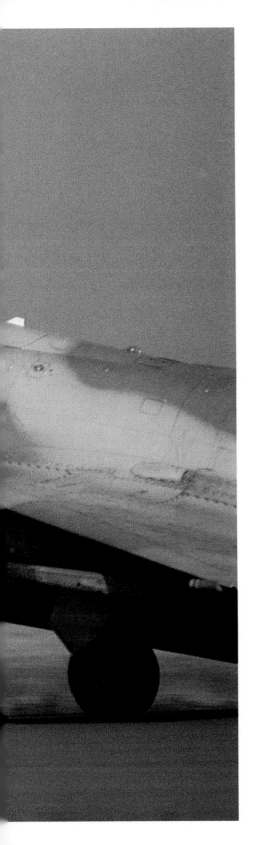

Approaching at 140 knots, '2-LO' recovers after an ACM sortie. The sortie being a resounding success, the pilot exuberantly keeps the power on and pops a perfectly controlled wheelie down the length of BA 102's runway. Whilst remaining full members of the North Atlantic Treaty Organisation (NATO), France withdrew its armed forces from the joint military command in 1966, feeling the Nation's best interests were served by retaining independent control. However, they still train with their allies, Mirage 2000 squadrons regularly dogfighting with other NATO aircraft in dissimilar air combat training

Keep 'em Flying

Below Often overshadowed by the 'glamorous' fighter jock, the men who keep their complex machines serviceable are a vital cog in the CAFDA 'works'. The fourth component of the 2nd *Escadre de Chasse* is their second line maintenance unit, the *Groupe d'entretien et réparation de matériel spécialisé* (GERMAS) 15.002 consisting of some 250 technicians who know the Mirage 2000 inside out. Here, jacked up and stripped down, an *'Alsace'* Mirage 2000C undergoes its routine three years or 900 hours deep maintenance overhaul

Right The GERMAS engine shop is equipped to handle both minor and major repairs to the SNECMA M53-5 or M53-P2. For ease of handling the engines can be up-ended on hydraulic lifts sunk into the floor and raised and lowered as necessary. Aside from remedial work, engines pass through the shop on routine 300 and 600 hour service cycles

Above Wired into the GERMAS 15.002's computerized test rig, a SNECMA
M53-P2 runs on full afterburner. This engine came from Luxeuil with a
compressor problem, and after repair was taken to Dijon's 'hush-house' for
comprehensive testing. The computer will analyse every aspect of the engine
performance, first at 4800 rpm idle speed, then 10,600 rpm full-power, and
finally with afterburner. Between each stage the computer spits out reams of
data and either recommends remedial action if a fault is discovered, or ok's the
next leg of the test

Right In the test-bed control room the noise level is a mere 40 decibels. The
engine can be seen but almost not heard through double glazing of two one and
half inch thick glass panels three feet apart

Left The deep maintenance sessions are a good opportunity for Dassault-Breguet and Thompson-CSF technicians to 'tweak', or incorporate, modifications into the complicated systems that pack the Mirage's slim body

Above Once the boffins have finished their work someone has to put the Mirage back together again!

Left Today's frontline fighters rely heavily on computers for almost every aspect of their operation. So, in the GERMAS complex at Dijon-Longvic there is a whole room stacked with computer hardware devoted to testing and rectifying any fault that might arise in the Mirage 2000's many 'black boxes'

Below Computerized audio-visual technology is used by the *Ensemble Mobile d'instruction* (EMI), who conduct various Mirage 2000 familiarization courses. All relevant personnel from groundcrew, through to technicians and pilots will attend for between three to eighteen weeks, depending upon their field of employment

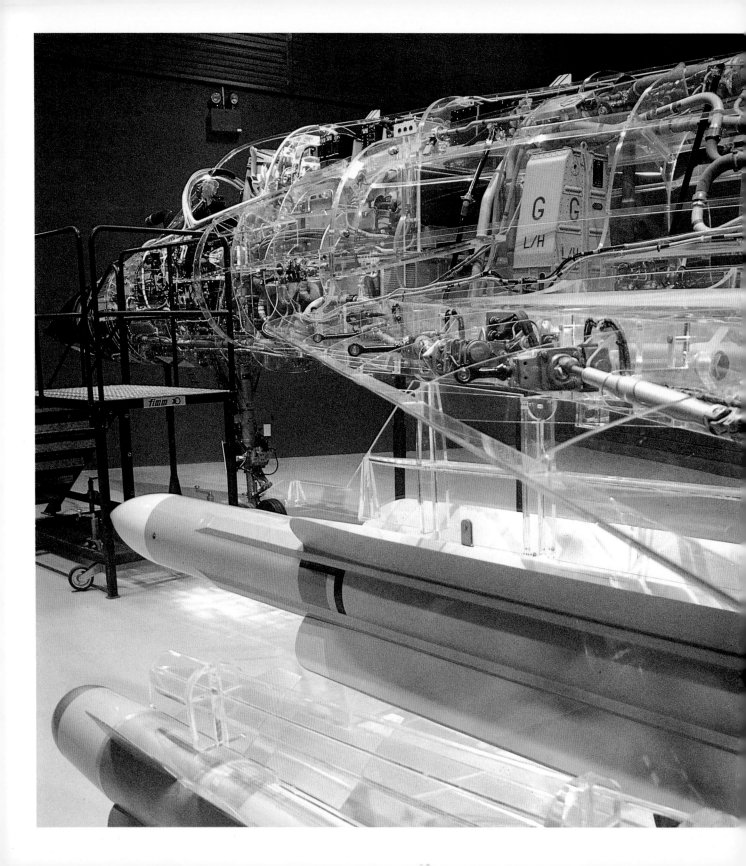

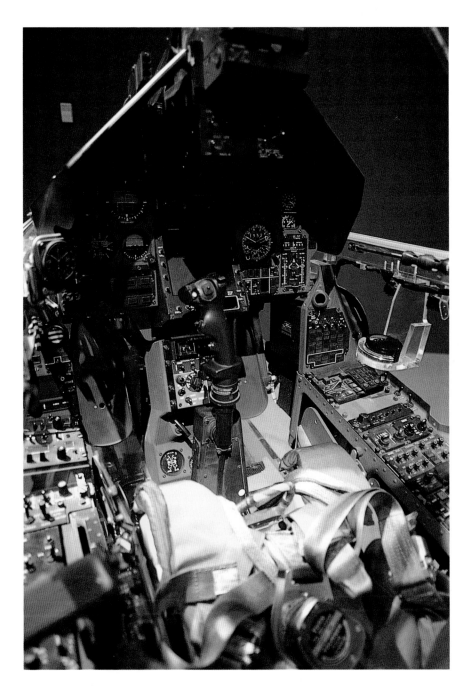

Opposite Originally constructed by Dassault-Breguet for the 1983 Paris Airshow, this full-size plexiglass Mirage 2000C was presented to BA 102 as an instructional aid and a 'thank you' for assistance given on the commercial front. Complete with Matra 550 Magic and Matra Super 530 air-to-air missiles, the 'Crystal Mirage', as it is known, is an impressive monument to the art of aviation design

Left The pilot's compact 'front office', packed with instruments and controls. In the centre is the cathode ray head-down display

In the EC 3/2 'Alsace' hangar a SNECMA M53-5 is shoehorned back into place after servicing in the GERMAS workshops. At the time of writing it is not expected that EC 2 aircraft will be retrofitted with the M53-P2 engine, although they will have their radar installations updated to the RDI

The finely engineered undercarriage is manufactured by Messier-Hispano-Bugatti, and vintage car buffs will immediately recognize two-thirds of the company name. What they might not know however, is that the designer of the engine that powered Georges Guynemer's SPAD in 1916, Marc Birkigt, was also co-founder and chief designer of the famous Hispano-Suiza car company. Further, he was so impressed by the *'Cigognes'* success with the SPAD that he adopted their stork emblem as a radiator mascot on post-war cars. It's been said that the mascot was as lethal to pedestrians as the *'Cigognes'* were to the enemy!

Above The business end of one of the DEFA 554 30 mm cannon fitted to the single-seat 2000C. Each cannon has a 125 round magazine

Right A close up of one of the four underwing pylons common to both Mirage 2000B and C variants. The safety clips are withdrawn as part of pre-fighting, and the yellow and black 'trigger' will be closed by airflow on take-off

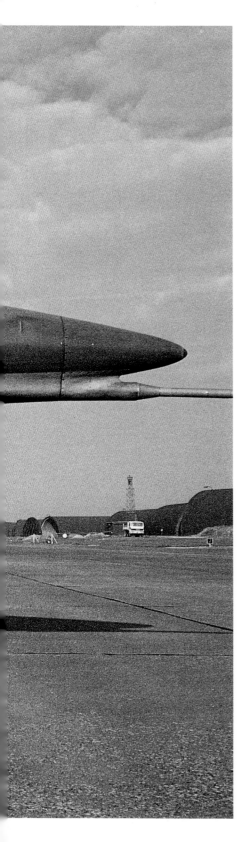

Fixed Wing Visitors

Left Cooling off on the Dijon flightline after flying in from Colmar, these Mirage 5Fs are starting to look their age. The Mirage 5 was originally developed when Dassault-Breguet identified a niche in the export market for a fair weather ground attack version of their best-selling Mirage IIIC. Basically this meant deleting the sophisticated radar and fire control equipment from the aircraft, and increasing it's internal fuel capacity and ordnance carrying capability. Israel was the first customer with an order for 50 of what was then designated the Mirage 5J. The prototype first flew on 19 May 1967, but the eruption of the Six Day War scarcely a month later caused France to place an embargo on all military material destined for Israel and the aircraft were never delivered

Below Political wrangling continued through 1968 but the Israeli raid on Beirut airport in January 1969 effectively closed negotiations. The 50 Mirage 5Js were impounded and Israel's payments returned. But the story didn't end there. Not to be outdone, Israel 'obtained' plans from a Swiss engineer and manufactured its own version! Eventually in 1972, after several years in storage, the 'tug-of-war Mirage 5Js' were re-designated 5Fs and entered *Armée de l'Air* service

Opposite above and below Whilst the pilots go off for a well earned break, Dijon groundcrew cluster around to re-aquaint themselves with the Mirage 5F's turnaround procedures. The first task for today is to attach pairs of inert 250 kg bombs to the dual role bomb launcher/fuel tanks. The Mirage 5F can carry up to 8820 lbs of ordnance and 220 gallons of fuel on its seven available hardpoints, and since these aircraft will give good service for several years to come groundgrew must remain current on the type

Above The colourful jester badge of *Escadrille* SPA 85 carried on the left fin side of EC 3/13 aircraft

Left 'Why are you interested in this old thing?' asks the pilot with a sideways, and possibly longing, look at the row of pristine Mirage 2000s parked not far away. The Mirage 5's SNECMA Atar 9C afterburning turbojet develops 13,670 pounds of thrust. Although this gives it a Mach two performance, it just doesn't compare with the 19,000 lbs plus produced by the newer M53 series engines powering the Mirage 2000

Above The '13' code on the nose of this Mirage 5F denotes its attachment to EC 3/13 '*Auvergne*'. In past lives '*Auvergne*' served in Morocco, Indo-China and Germany, before being disbanded in 1965. They were reformed at Colmar on 1 May 1972 and were the first squadron to receive the Mirage 5F, an aircraft they are likely to operate well into the 1990s

Right An *Aéronavale* Dassault-Breguet Super Étendard of 11 *Flotille* based at Landivisiau. But for a twist of fate this type might have served its time and disappeared into history as an 'also ran', overshadowed by its Mirage stablemates. However, the words 'combat proven' in Dassault's publicity material reminds us that the Super Étendard, when flown by the Argentinian Navy and armed with the deadly Exocet AM 39 air-to-surface missile, destroyed the Royal Navy destroyer HMS *Sheffield* and the merchant ship *Atlantic Conveyor* during the 1982 Falklands campaign. In 1986, this time in Iraqi hands, the same aircraft/missile combination wrought havoc in the Persian Gulf

Above Head-on, the resemblance to the Mirage family is apparent. The Super Étendard is a carrier or ground based multi-role single-seater powered by the SNECMA Atar 8K-50 turbojet, a non-afterburning version of the 9K-50 that powers some Mirage III/50 variants. This pilot looks a little weary as he waits for the Dijon groundcrew to find an access ladder. No doubt he's impatient to sample the excellent officer's mess fare

Below Having its 3270 litre internal fuel load topped up, this Super Étendard is lightly laden with only a pair of external fuel tanks under its wings. The type can carry a wide range of ordnance from the ASMP nuclear missile, through to Matra 550 Magic AAMs, bombs, rocket launchers and the infamous Exocet AM 39-mix and match to a total of 4630 lbs! All of that is in addition to the twin DEFA 152 30 mm cannon with 125 rounds a piece mounted in the wings

Opposite above The *Aéronavale* seahorse badge of the 11 *Flotille* (squadron). Eleven F has existed in various guises since 1926, over the years operating such types as the Seafire, Hellcat, Aquilon (Sea Venom) and Étendard, before receiving the Super Étendard in 1978. Current base is Landivisiau, in Brittany, where they have been since May 1967

Right Glad to get out of his G-suit, the pilot dangles it from a convenient, but unauthorised, hanger whilst he and the groundcrewman make a quick walk-around check. The Super Étendard is vastly superior to the original Étendard IVM which it has replaced, particularly in the area of weapons delivery. It has Thomson-CSF Agave multi-mode radar for air-to-air, air-to-sea and air-to-ground engagements, plus an inertial navigation system and head-up display

Above The distinctively profiled nose identifies this as an Étendard IVP photo-reconnaissance aircraft. The Étendard was originally developed in the mid-fifties in the hope of being accepted as a standard NATO light strike fighter. In the ensuing competition it was bested by the Fiat G.91, but luckily for Dassault the *Aéronavale* came forward with orders for the IVM carrier based light strike variant and the IVP reconnaissance version

Opposite above The Étendard IVP is unarmed and mounts five Omera cameras behind optically flat glass windows; three in the nose and two in the belly. The prototype Étendard IV strike fighter flew on 24 July 1956, but it was not until 19 November 1960 that the first IVP version was flown. The production model Étendard IVM strike fighter has been superceded by the Super Étendard, but the IVP soldiers on

Opposite below Otherwise devoid of serials or code numbers, the '109' identifies this Étendard IVP as belonging to Landivisiau based 16 *Flotille*. The IVP is powered by the 9700 lb thrust SNECMA Atar 9B, and is likely to remain in service until replaced by the vastly superior Rafale B. Exactly when this is to take place is currently open to conjecture

Previous pages At Dijon to pick up
and transport EC 1/2 *'Cigognes'*
spares and baggage to Istres in
support of a two-week exercise, this
Transall C-160F is one of the second
series batch which started to come off
the production line in 1976. In January
1959 the Transall (Transporter
Allianz) group was formed to develop
and manufacture a military transport
aircraft to meet the needs of both
Federal Germany and France. The
prototype, designated C-160 because
of the 160 square metre wing area,
first flew in February 1963

Right First series production closed
in 1972 after a total of 169 had been
produced, but an *Armée de l'Air*
requirement for a further 29 aircraft
started the production lines rolling
again at Aérospatiale and MBB in
1977. Updated avionics are a feature
of the second series, with the
compact flight deck being
particularly well laid out

Right Groundcrew manhandle a pallet stacked with Mirage 2000 wheels and other spare parts under the C-160's high swept tail

Above Link pallet to runners on the loading ramp and the cargo can be slid directly into the C-160's cavernous pressurized interior. The Transall's sturdy undercarriage, which consists of tandem pairs of wheels in sponsons, is designed for use on poorly prepared surfaces, and can 'kneel' to ease loading via the rear ramp

The Mission

Left A distinctive feature of the second series C-160 Transall is an in-flight refuelling probe mounted above the flightdeck. The aircraft benefit from a strengthened wing with the option of an additional fuel tank mounted in its centre section. Since there are only so many ways to configure a military transporter it is hardly suprising that the Transall bears a marked resemblance to Lockheed's C-130 Hercules, but with only two engines – Rolls-Royce Tyne Mk 22 turboprops

Army Transients

Left Photographed during a refuelling stop at Dijon, this pair of *Armée de Terre* SA.330B Pumas from the 7th *Régiment d'Hélicoptères de Combat* (RHC) are on their way from Etain to Roussen to collect a detachment of troops. Each can carry up to 20 passengers or a maximum cargo load of 7055 lbs. There are two RHCs attached to each of the two army corps and a further two RHCs held in reserve

Below The Puma was originally developed by Sud-Aviation, now known as Aérospatiale, to meet an *Aviation Légère de l'Armée de Terre* requirement for an all-weather medium transport helicopter. The prototype flew on 15 April 1965, but before the first production model took to the air in September 1968 the Puma had been ordered by the Royal Air Force and became part of an Anglo-French production programme

Above This example of the Puma 330B is painted in the usual *Armée de Terre* olive drab, with national roundels, and the last three letters of the callsign. No unit markings are worn

Left Fuel tanks full, the Puma pair stand evocatively silhouetted in the weak winter sunlight as they prepare to leave Dijon and head south

Above The three-man crew of 'BUS' scan their instrument panel before starting the pair of Turboméca Turmo IIIC4 turboshafts mounted forward of the rotor hub

Left This Puma's North African/Chad style camouflage is less than suitable for operations over the lush green vineyards of Burgundy

Above With the leading machine shimmering in the heat of its own exhaust, and their great 15 metre diameter blades noisily chopping the air, the pair of Pumas taxi away for take-off

Right Another pair of 7th *Régiment d'Hélicoptères de Combat* machines avail themselves of BA 102 hospitality. In the foreground is an Alouette III and to the rear a Aérospatiale SA.341 Gazelle. The streamlined shape of the Gazelle illustrates the decade separating their basic designs

Below As mist starts to roll across the base the race is on to refuel and leave Dijon before visibility deteriorates too far

Right 'Hey, watch the paintwork!' says the Alouette pilot as his machine's fuel tank is filled to overflowing

Above The Sud-Aviation Alouette III was derived from the smaller open-bodied Alouette II, and the prototype flew on 28 February 1959. Built in their thousands in France, India, Rumania and Switzerland, various versions of the type are operated by well over fifty air arms around the world

Left Although distantly related to the Alouette, the Gazelle's streamlined and stressed-skin fuselage makes for an altogether more attractive design. The prototype SA.340's maiden flight was in April 1967, but there were problems and it took until August 1971 for the production configuration (semi-articulated main rotor and 'fenestron' tail) to evolve as the SA.341 seen here

Above An unusual feature of the Gazelle, and several other Aérospatiale designs, is the shrouded tail rotor, known as a 'fenestron'

Right The Gazelle's cabin features side-by-side seating for the crew, with dual controls and a superb all-round view

Base Alert

Left Wander the flightline without the correct authority and you'll very soon find yourself face to face with the men (and dogs) of BA 102's commando unit, a tough looking bunch if ever there was one

Below 0500 hours and the base is put on alert. Offbase personnel are recalled, operational areas sealed tight as a drum, and the armoured cars of the *Section de défense sol-air* (SDSA) rumble around the perimeter from watchtower to watchtower

Swiftly the SDSA deploy their 20 mm anti-aircraft guns at strategic points around the base and man them throughout the miserably damp November morning

Right Adjutant Ramires keeps his cool whilst one of the 35 dogs in his charge demonstrates exactly why BA 102 would have no trouble dealing with intruders. Ideally dogs will start their training at about eight to ten months of age and take a further eight to ten months to reach operational standard. During that time they will be paired with one handler to build a mutual relationship of trust and respect

Above Teamwork is the name of the game. Having caught an 'intruder', the guard-dog looks on with a 'make my day' expression as his handler searches for weapons

Above Fitness is always a service priority and an early morning jog past the still closed maintenance sheds is sheer pleasure on a day like this

Right Having pulled early watch in the control tower on a crisp misty morning there isn't much to do except discuss the weather situation with the pilot of an incoming Fouga Magister

Magister

Right Better known for their character rather than their good looks are the Fouga Magister CM 170s operated by BA 102's communication flight, *Section accruel de liasons d'entrainement* (SALE). Production examples of this basic tandem two-seater first flew in 1956 and over 900 were built in various forms before the lines closed in 1969

Below The mirror-like shine on the wings indicate the amount of loving care bestowed on these senior citizens. The basic CM 170s flown by SALE are powered by two 882 lb thrust Marboré IIA turbojets, though there were more potently engined variants produced

Above From the front and in a flattering light the Magister looks almost elegant, the slim fuselage cleanly tapering off to the aircraft's 'trademark', the butterfly wing tail surfaces. Not so long ago an unusual tailplane configuration, but currently back in vogue with aircraft designers for it's stealth value, it is doubtful whether the Fouga designers were aware of that aspect when they pencilled together the Magister!

Left The pilot of a 12th *Escadre* CM 170 over from Cambrai on routine inter-base duties exchanges a word with the Dijon groundcrew before climbing into his aircraft's rather basic cockpit

Left The Magister sits unusually low to the ground on the short tricycle undercarriage, and the angle iron airbrakes protruding from the wing are a quaint touch. Aesthetic peculiarities aside, the sheer number built and the fact that so many are still flying is ample evidence of a sound design

Below 'Is there a problem?' asks the pilot. There certainly is! As the crew vacate their cockpit the groundcrew gaze disconsolately at the growing puddle of fuel under the Magister's fuselage. Press down on the tail to tip the nose up and the trickle becomes a flood. Not something to try with a Mirage!

Into the air and the ugly duckling becomes a swan. The flying qualities of the Magister are confirmed by it's selection over the years for the national aerobatic display teams of France, Belgium, Brazil, West Germany and Israel. The *Armée de l'Air* use their surviving examples in a pilot training role and as liason aircraft. This BA 102 'base hack' bears the SALE badge, a combination of 2nd *Escadre* squadron colours and insignia

Ivan, Check Six!

Left Nose art has no place on today's sleek *Armée de l'Air* fighters but custom painted helmets are definitely the fashion for French 'Top Guns'. On the front of the helmet perhaps just the pilot's name and flight insignia, but on the back . . .

Below . . . anything goes. This beautiful example of the art was created by Dijon's airbrush maestro, Sergent Thierry Brabant, for a pilot flying Mirage F.1s out of Cambrai

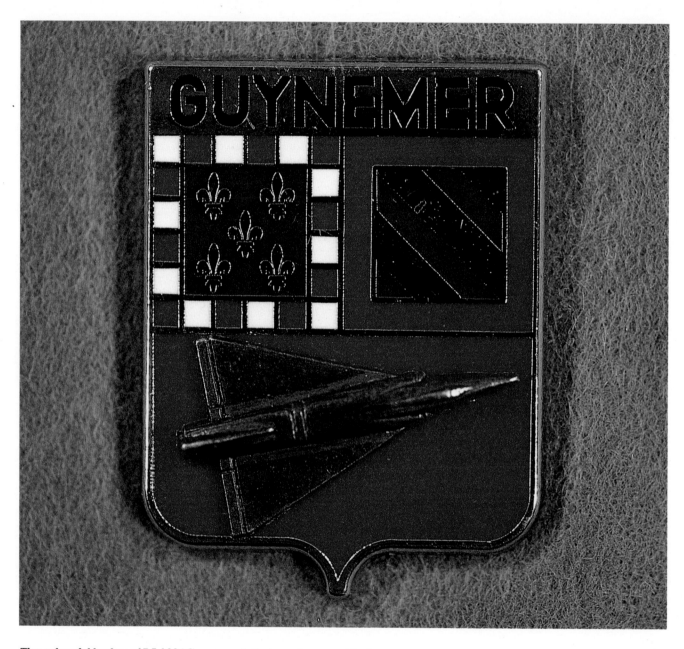

The colourful badge of BA 102 'Guynemer'. Past meets present in the combination of the coat of arms of the Dukes of Bourgogne and the Mirage delta